ECOFACTS

BIODIVERSITY

ECO FACTS

IZZI HOWELL

CRABTREE
PUBLISHING COMPANY
WWW.CRABTREEBOOKS.COM

CRABTREE
PUBLISHING COMPANY
WWW.CRABTREEBOOKS.COM

Author: Izzi Howell

Editorial director: Kathy Middleton

Editors: Izzi Howell, Ellen Rodger

Proofreader: Melissa Boyce

Designer: Clare Nicholas

Cover designer: Steve Mead

Prepress technician: Tammy McGarr

Print coordinator: Katherine Berti

Photo credits:
Alamy: Zizza Gordon Wildlife Collection 13t; Getty: James_Gabbert 8, David Butler 9b, Eco Images 11t, MikeLane45 15, pierivb 18, byakkaya 19, Stockbyte 20, ad_foto 21, duncan1890 29; Shutterstock: Swapan Photography 7, Rich Carey 9t, KYTan 10, Keith Homan 11b, Tom Brakefield 13b, Iurii Kazakov 14, Tom Grundy 16, Mr F 23, Michael Fitzsimmons 24, David Osborn 27.

All design elements from Shutterstock.

Every attempt has been made to clear copyright. Should there be any inadvertent omission please apply to the publisher for rectification.

The website addresses (URLs) included in this book were valid at the time of going to press. However, it is possible that contents or addresses may have changed since the publication of this book. No responsibility for any such changes can be accepted by either the author or the Publisher.

Library and Archives Canada Cataloguing in Publication

Title: Biodiversity eco facts / Izzi Howell.
Names: Howell, Izzi, author.
Description: Series statement: Eco facts | Includes index.
Identifiers: Canadiana (print) 20190087994 |
  Canadiana (ebook) 20190088001 |
  ISBN 9780778763444 (hardcover) |
  ISBN 9780778763567 (softcover) |
  ISBN 9781427123428 (HTML)
Subjects: LCSH: Biodiversity—Juvenile literature. |
  LCSH: Nature—Effect of human beings on—Juvenile   literature.
Classification: LCC QH541.15.B56 H69 2019 |
  DDC j333.95—dc23

Library of Congress Cataloging-in-Publication Data

Names: Howell, Izzi, author.
Title: Biodiversity eco facts / Izzi Howell.
Description: New York, New York : Crabtree Publishing, 2019. |
Series: Eco facts | Includes index. |
Identifiers: LCCN 2019014529 (print) | LCCN 2019019418 (ebook) |
  ISBN 9781427123428 (Electronic) |
  ISBN 9780778763444 (hardcover : alk. paper) |
  ISBN 9780778763567 (pbk. : alk. paper)
Subjects: LCSH: Biodiversity--Juvenile literature.
Classification: LCC QH541.15.B56 (ebook) |
  LCC QH541.15.B56 H68 2019 (print) | DDC 333.95--dc23
LC record available at https://lccn.loc.gov/2019014529

Crabtree Publishing Company

www.crabtreebooks.com   1–800–387–7650

Published by Crabtree Publishing Company in 2020
©2019 The Watts Publishing Group.

Printed in the U.S.A./072019/CG20190501

Published in Canada
Crabtree Publishing
616 Welland Ave.
St. Catharines, Ontario
L2M 5V6

Published in the United States
Crabtree Publishing
PMB 59051
350 Fifth Avenue, 59th Floor
New York, New York 10118

Contents

What is biodiversity?

A huge variety of different types of plants and animals live on Earth. We use the word biodiversity—a combination of the words biological and **diversity**—to describe this variety.

Types of biodiversity

There are three types of biodiversity:

- Genetic: Animals and plants of the same **species** can have slightly different genes
- Species: A variety of species live in all the different habitats and **ecosystems** on Earth
- Ecosystem: There are also many different types of ecosystems on Earth

Genetic biodiversity

Importance

All types of biodiversity—genetic, species, and ecosystem—are important. Genetic diversity helps keep species healthy and **resistant** to disease or climate change. Species diversity is important for food chains in ecosystems. If one species is lost, every species will be affected. Ecosystem diversity supports millions of different animal and plant species.

Around 1.9 million species have been recorded on Earth. There are probably around 8–9 million in total!

Humans

Humans benefit from biodiversity. We rely on plants and animals for food, medicine, and construction, among many other uses. Plants also help to maintain oxygen in the atmosphere. Some people also believe that we should protect biodiversity because humans have a moral responsibility to look after Earth.

Ecosystem biodiversity

At risk

Extinctions and habitat destruction can happen naturally. Throughout Earth's history, there have been five mass extinctions. These happened naturally, due to volcanic eruptions, ice ages, and meteor impacts. Some scientists believe we are entering a sixth mass extinction, caused by humans. Humans are the biggest threat to biodiversity today.

Many types of dinosaurs became extinct during a mass extinction 65 million years ago. It was thought to have been caused when a giant meteor hit Earth.

Genetic diversity

All members of a species have mostly the same **DNA** (genetic information). However, there is also some diversity in DNA, which helps species to survive.

Small differences

It's easy to see small differences in DNA in humans. Our physical characteristics, such as skin color, hair color, and risk of developing certain diseases, change from person to person. However, nearly all our DNA—around 99.9 percent—is the same.

Animal differences

All living things have genetic diversity. Just like humans, some members of a species may look slightly different or be naturally resistant to a disease. These differences can happen randomly or they can be passed down from parent to child.

Natural selection

Genetic diversity helps animals and plants to evolve, or change for the better over time. This happens through a process called natural selection.

1 Some members of a species may randomly have a genetic advantage. For example, they may not catch a certain disease, while others do.

2 The ones who do not catch the disease are more likely to survive and **reproduce**, passing on their DNA to the next generation.

3 Over time, more and more members of the species will be born with the helpful genetic difference.

Habitat adaptations

Species adapt to their habitat through natural selection. If a member of a species is born with an advantage, such as thick fur in a cold habitat, they will be more likely to survive and pass on this advantage. Animals continue to evolve as their habitats change. In this way, some animals will be able to survive changes in their habitat, such as **global warming**.

GM crops

Scientists can change the DNA of certain plants to make them more useful to humans. They are called genetically modified (GM) crops. For example, the bananas that we eat have been changed so that they don't have seeds. This makes them nicer to eat.

This wild banana contains many seeds.

Cloning

Some GM crops, such as bananas, can't reproduce naturally because they don't have seeds. Instead, they are cloned—genetically identical copies of each other are made. This means that there is no genetic diversity. If a new disease attacked bananas, none of the bananas would be naturally resistant to it. This means that the entire species could die out.

Inbreeding

If there is only a small population of a species, there is less genetic diversity. This means that any genetic problems are more likely to spread and affect more of the species. Having closely related parents can lead to genetic and health problems for plants and animals. This is why genetic diversity is important.

Ecosystems

An ecosystem is made up of all the living things in an area. Every animal and plant in an ecosystem depends on the other species living there to survive. If one species disappears or experiences a change in population, the whole ecosystem will be affected.

Food chains

The species in an ecosystem depend on each other for food. The plants provide food for herbivores. The herbivores, or prey animals, are then eaten by carnivores. Carnivores are predators, who may then be eaten by bigger predators. We can show the prey and predators in an ecosystem in a food chain.

Bluebirds are omnivores that eat both plants and animals, such as grasshoppers. Snakes are carnivores that eat bluebirds. Owls are also carnivores that eat snakes.

Ecosystem relationships

Species in an ecosystem affect each other in many ways. Insects help to **pollinate** flowering plants, which allows the plants to reproduce and create seeds (see page 25). Some animals help to spread plant seeds by carrying them on their fur or in their waste. Other animals help to control their environment by cutting down plants or digging holes.

Beavers cut down trees and plants and use them to build dams on rivers. These dams create different wetland habitats for other species.

Keystone species

Keystone species are very important in an ecosystem. A keystone is the central stone in an arch. If the keystone is removed, the whole arch falls apart. Keystone species are the same. If they disappeared, the entire ecosystem would fall apart.

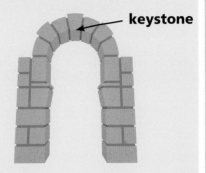

keystone

Parrotfish

Parrotfish are keystone species in coral reefs. They eat algae, which grows on coral. When the number of parrotfish decreases, the amount of algae covering coral increases, which makes the coral grow more slowly. Without parrotfish, coral reefs are not able to grow properly.

Parrotfish use their sharp teeth to scrape algae off coral and rocks.

Prairie dogs

Prairie dogs are keystone species on the prairie grasslands of North America. They dig large underground burrows, where they sleep and hide from predators. These burrows are useful to the prairie ecosystem in many ways. They are used as shelter by other animals. Rainwater is absorbed quickly into the ground through the burrows. Keeping the ground moist helps reduce **erosion**.

Prairie dogs build their burrows close together in groups called towns.

Deforestation

Humans are cutting down huge areas of forest. In doing so, they are destroying some of the most biodiverse areas on Earth.

Reasons

Some trees are cut down for timber to be used in building or furniture. Other areas of forest are cleared to build roads or so that the land can be used for farming. Many forests are cut down to grow soybeans and palm trees for oil, or to raise cattle for their meat.

A rain forest in Malaysia has been cleared for this palm-oil farm.

Rainforest biodiversity

Deforestation is a serious problem in tropical rain forests in South America, Africa, and South Asia. Rain forests contain around 80 percent of all recorded species on Earth. When this habitat is destroyed through deforestation, this huge biodiversity is lost.

In one 0.025 square miles (0.06 sq km) of rain forest in Borneo, 700 species of trees have been recorded. That is the same number of species as in the whole of North America.

Hidden treasures

Many medicines have been developed from rainforest plants. Scientists worry that deforestation may destroy an unknown plant that could become a life-saving medicine. So far, only 0.5 percent of flowering plants have been studied to see if they could be used as medicines.

Saving the trees

One way to protect rain forests is to create protected areas where trees can't be cut down. This is helping to protect areas of the Amazon rain forest (see pages 12–13). We can also **boycott** products that are often grown on deforested land, such as palm oil.

Native trees can be replanted in deforested areas. However, it can take a long time for the animals and plant species to return to the ecosystem.

Solving the problem

There is more to deforestation than saving trees. Farmland is needed to produce food to support Earth's growing population. People who live near forests depend on timber or land-clearing for income. We need to invest in different farming methods and alternative jobs for these people, to solve the problem of deforestation in the long term.

One small step

Look for the Rainforest Alliance logo when shopping. Products with this logo have been grown in a way that does not damage rain forests.

The Amazon rain forest

The Amazon rain forest is the world's largest tropical rain forest. It is also one of the most biodiverse places on Earth, containing around 10 percent of the world's biodiversity.

FACT FILE

LOCATION:
South America

SIZE:
2.1 million square miles (5.5 million sq km)

THREATS:
Deforestation, poaching, **climate change**

In the Amazon rain forest, scientists have so far recorded:

1,300 bird species

427 mammal species

over 400 amphibian species

2.5 million insect species

Between 2014 and 2015, a new species was discovered in the Amazon every two days!

400,000 plant species

So many species

There are many species in the Amazon because each layer of the rain forest provides a different habitat. For example, the forest floor is dark and damp, while the top layer of the trees, the canopy, is bright and filled with branches. Over time, animals and plants have adapted to these conditions, creating new species in every layer.

These species of anteater have adapted to life in different rainforest ecosystems.

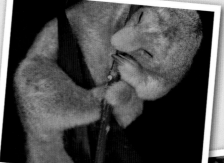

Silky anteaters (left) live high in the canopy layer. Their tail is flexible and can grip branches, which allows them to climb and swing from trees.

Giant anteaters (right) live on the forest floor. Their large bushy tail provides balance so they can stand on two legs to reach food.

Deforestation

Deforestation is the greatest threat to the Amazon rain forest. Over 17 percent of the tree cover has been destroyed in the past 50 years. The populations of recorded species such as the jaguar, the white-cheeked spider monkey, and some types of orchid have already been affected.

Medicines

Humans benefit from the biodiversity of plants that live in the Amazon. Scientists have developed medicines from certain species, such as a muscle relaxant from the bark of a vine. They are also developing new medicines. They think that the fungi that grow on sloths' fur could be used to treat breast cancer and malaria.

Saving the Amazon

Since 2000, huge sections of the Amazon rain forest have been turned into protected areas where trees can't be cut down. Deforestation rates have dropped as a result. However, these areas are not guaranteed protection forever. Charities, politicians, and celebrities take part in campaigns to raise awareness and pressure South American governments to continue protecting the rain forest.

Climate change

Many different habitats around the world are changing as a result of global warming. This has a ripple effect on the species that live there.

Global warming

The climate on Earth is getting warmer and wetter. Most scientists agree that this is because of human activity. Burning oil, coal, and natural gas, traveling by car or plane, and **livestock** farming all create **greenhouse gases**, such as carbon dioxide. Greenhouse gases gather in the atmosphere and trap heat from the Sun close to Earth. This makes the temperature rise on Earth.

Emperor penguins come on to the ice to rest and keep safe from predators in the water, such as leopard seals.

The poles

The rising temperature on Earth is causing ice to melt at the poles. This is destroying the habitat of animals that spend time on the ice, such as emperor penguins. Emperor penguins breed on sea ice. They also rest on the ice while hunting for fish underwater.

Rising sea levels

Melting ice at the poles is adding more water into Earth's oceans. This is making sea levels rise around the world. Coastal habitats, such as tide pools, are at risk. Animals that hunt for food in wetlands by the coast, such as seabirds, are finding it harder to feed themselves as the sea covers their hunting grounds.

Acid oceans

The oceans absorb some of the extra carbon dioxide in the atmosphere. This makes the ocean water more acidic. Acidic water damages the shells of shellfish and crabs. It also dissolves coral and stops it from growing. This is a serious problem, as coral is the habitat of many ocean animals and plants.

Life cycles

The warmer temperatures are affecting life cycles around the world. Plants are flowering and producing fruit earlier in the year. Animals are also breeding and giving birth earlier. Animals that **migrate** for food or to avoid cold weather are moving at different times.

Butterflies are reproducing four days earlier every 10 years!

Changing behavior

Changes in behavior caused by climate change are throwing ecosystems out of balance. If plants flower too early, the insects needed to pollinate them may not be around. This means that plants will not be able to reproduce and create fruit and seeds. Animals that migrate for food may starve if they arrive before or after the food source is ready.

The pied flycatcher migrates to Europe in spring to eat newly hatched insects. However, its population has been decreasing recently, as insects have been hatching earlier, before the pied flycatchers arrive.

Pollution

Waste created by humans is polluting different habitats around the world. This pollution threatens the species that live there.

Oil spills

Oil often spills out of oil wells at sea, as well as out of ships transporting oil to land. The oil covers ocean mammals and birds, making it hard for them to stay warm and float in the water. When these animals clean themselves, they eat the oil, which can poison them. Oil also poisons fish and shellfish.

Plastic

Plastic waste is a risk to animals on land and in the sea. Animals often eat small pieces of plastic, mistaking them for food. This plastic can damage the insides of the animals and eventually kill them. Animals can also get their legs and heads trapped in pieces of plastic, which makes it hard for them to move and swim.

This seagull is trapped in plastic packaging for cans.

In the Exxon Valdez oil spill in 1989, more than **11 million gallons** (42 million L) of oil spilled off the coast of Alaska. The oil spill killed:

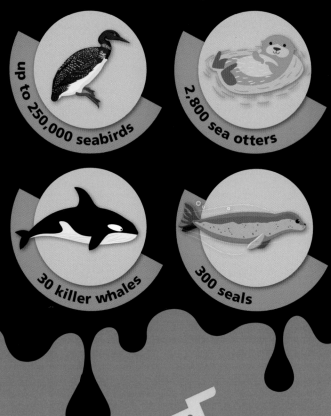

up to 250,000 seabirds

2,800 sea otters

30 killer whales

300 seals

Acid rain

When **fossil fuels** such as coal and oil are burned, they release gases that mix with water in the atmosphere. This creates acid rain, which damages plants and soil when it falls to the ground. It removes nutrients from the soil and damages plants' leaves.

Chemicals

Some farmers use chemicals when growing crops. They use **fertilizers** to add more nutrients to the soil and **pesticides** to kill insects that eat the crops. However, these chemicals can harm other species that live near the crops, such as frogs. Insects that pollinate crops, such as bees (see page 25), are often accidentally killed by pesticides. When fertilizers are washed into rivers and lakes, they make too much algae grow, which blocks light from reaching other underwater plants.

Organic farming

Organic farming is one way of protecting animals from dangerous chemicals. On organic farms, farmers do not use any artificial chemicals, such as fertilizers and pesticides. Around 50 percent more wild animals and plants live on organic farms than on standard farms, which helps to improve biodiversity.

One small step

Try to buy organic food when possible. You could also grow your own fruit and vegetables without pesticides.

Hunting

Most of the animals that humans use for meat or resources are raised on farms. However, we still hunt some wild animals, both legally and illegally.

Fish

Fish are the most commonly caught wild animals. Many people around the world depend on wild fish for food.

Overfishing

Sometimes, fishers catch too many fish. This often happens as a result of trawler fishing, in which fishers use huge nets to catch anything in their path. They don't leave enough of a species to breed, so the population can't recover. Over time, the population decreases. This has happened with species such as cod and Atlantic bluefin tuna.

Ocean ecosystems

When the population of one species of fish decreases, it affects the entire ocean ecosystem. Large predators such as dolphins, which depend on the fish for food, can't get enough food to thrive. The animals normally eaten by the fish increase in population, changing the ecosystem.

Supporting people

Overfishing affects people who depend on fish for food and income. It may seem as if fishing without limits is a good idea, as people can make more money. However, it actually threatens people's future income, as it doesn't leave enough fish to catch and sell. It's important to encourage **sustainable** fishing, in which people can catch enough to support themselves, and fish populations are protected for the future.

A woman in Madagascar, Africa, collects recently caught fish on the beach.

Poaching

Some wild animals are hunted or captured illegally. This is called poaching. Some commonly poached animals include the black rhino, the mountain gorilla, and the African elephant.

Traditional medicine

Rhinos are often illegally hunted for their horns, which are used in some forms of traditional medicine. Other ingredients in traditional medicine that come from poached animals include water buffalo horns, tiger bones, and sun bear gallbladders.

Since 2007, more than 7,900 African rhinos have been lost to poaching

Illegal luxury items

There is a demand for luxury items that come from animals. Tigers and leopards are hunted illegally for their fur. Some species of snakes and monkeys are caught and sold as pets. These animals and products sell for a high price around the world.

At some tourist attractions, people pay money to pose in photos with cute animals that have been poached, such as this slow loris.

Alternative income

Poaching is often carried out by organized criminal gangs in poorer countries. One way to stop poachers is to create other ways to make money in these areas, such as safari parks. Animals in safari parks are worth more alive than dead, as tourists pay to see them in the wild.

The ivory trade

Ivory is a hard, white material. It comes from the tusks of elephants and walruses, and the teeth of some animals, such as hippopotamuses. The demand for ivory threatens these species.

History

In the past, ivory was very popular. It was used to make ornaments, jewelry, and furniture. These ivory objects were often carved with intricate designs.

Finding ivory

Ivory can be taken from animals that died of natural causes. However, the demand in the 1800s and 1900s was so high that poachers began to kill animals, especially African elephants, for their tusks. This led to a rapid decrease in the elephant population.

Ivory ban

The trade in ivory from African elephants was banned worldwide in 1989. This ban was designed to help the elephant population recover. However, illegal poaching continues. There is still a high demand for ivory from countries such as China. Some countries, including the U.K., have banned the import of all ivory of any age to discourage poachers.

Workers in Africa count ivory tusks confiscated from poachers.

Keystone species

The African elephant is a keystone species in the savanna (see page 9). It uproots trees and shrubs, which stops forests from growing on these grasslands. It digs holes, which fill with rainwater that other animals can drink. Its waste even helps to spread seeds. If the African elephant became extinct, the savanna habitat would dramatically change, affecting all the other species that live there.

Alternatives

There are alternatives to killing live animals for ivory. There are around 10 million mammoths that have been frozen in ice in Russia for thousands of years. Ivory could be taken from these mammoths' tusks. There is also a type of seed that can be carved to look just like ivory.

This turtle statue looks like ivory, but it is actually carved from a seed.

The future

Some African countries want to start trading ivory again. They claim that the population of African elephants has recovered and is stable. The ivory trade could help to boost the economy in these countries. However, legalizing the ivory trade in some countries could encourage illegal poaching in other areas, as poachers will smuggle illegal ivory into these countries to sell it legally.

Invasive species

When plants and animals move into new habitats, it affects the biodiversity of the species that already live there. Sometimes, it increases biodiversity. But more often, it upsets the balance of the ecosystem.

Polar bears are moving south into forests, looking for food.

On the move

Some animals move into new areas as their population grows. If there isn't enough food in one area, the species spreads out. Many species of animal are also moving because of global warming. As their habitat changes with the climate, they move to new areas and slowly adapt to new habitats.

Growing in numbers

When a species is introduced to a new habitat, its population often increases quickly. There may be less competition with other animals for food. They may have no natural predators. This often affects native animals in the habitat who depend on the food supply or who are now eaten by the introduced animal.

When rabbits were first introduced to Australia in the 1800s, the population grew out of control because they had no natural predators.

Islands

Many islands are home to species that don't live anywhere else. This is because the ocean acts as a natural barrier, stopping species from reaching the island. However, humans have introduced animals to islands accidentally and on purpose.

On purpose

Humans have been deliberately introducing animals to new areas, such as islands, for thousands of years. In some cases, they wanted to introduce wild animals that they could hunt for food, such as rabbits. In other cases, they introduced a new species to solve an environmental problem. In Australia, cane toads were introduced to eat insects that damaged sugarcane crops.

Cane toads have seriously affected native biodiversity in Australia, as many animals die after coming into contact with the toad's poison.

By mistake

Some animals have been introduced to new areas accidentally. When sailors traveled to remote islands on ships, the mice and rats that lived below deck went with them. Mice and rats had no natural predators on these islands, so they quickly grew in number. In many cases, they affected the population of birds that nested on the ground, such as albatrosses, by eating their eggs.

Consequences

The loss of biodiversity is a serious risk to our planet.
When animals and plants disappear, it has serious
consequences for the natural world and for humans.

Extinction

When the last member of a species dies, that
species becomes extinct. Of all the species that
have ever lived, most are now extinct, largely
due to natural causes. However, human activity is
now the main cause of most animal extinctions.

**99.9 percent of all species
that ever lived are extinct.**

Extinct in the wild

Some animals are extinct in the wild. The only known living
members of their species live in zoos or wildlife reserves.
One day, it may be safe for the species to be reintroduced
to their habitat (see page 27). However, if their habitat
has been destroyed, this may never be possible.

*The Guam kingfisher is now extinct in the wild. Its population
was wiped out by a new species of snake that was
accidentally brought to the island on a ship in the 1950s.*

CO2

Climate change

The loss of plants has a negative impact on the
environment. Plants absorb carbon dioxide from the
atmosphere as part of their process of making energy.
If the number of plants goes down, there will be more
carbon dioxide in the atmosphere. This will increase the
greenhouse effect and make global warming worse.

CO2

Ocean barriers

Some ocean habitats protect the land from storms and flooding. Natural barriers in the water, such as coral reefs and wetlands, slow down ocean storms as they move towards land. If these habitats are lost because of pollution or ocean acidification, it can make weather and flooding worse along the coast.

Food supply

Our food supply is threatened by the loss of biodiversity. If we continue to fish in an unsustainable way, ocean ecosystems will collapse. We won't be able to depend on fish for food.

Bees

Bees play an important role in the life cycle of plants. They visit flowers, collecting pollen and nectar for food. Pollen sticks to their bodies and they carry it from one flower to another. This pollinates the flowers so that they can produce fruit and seeds. If we continue to use pesticides that kill bees, crops won't be pollinated and plants won't produce food for us to eat.

If bees disappeared, the life cycle of flowering plants couldn't be completed.

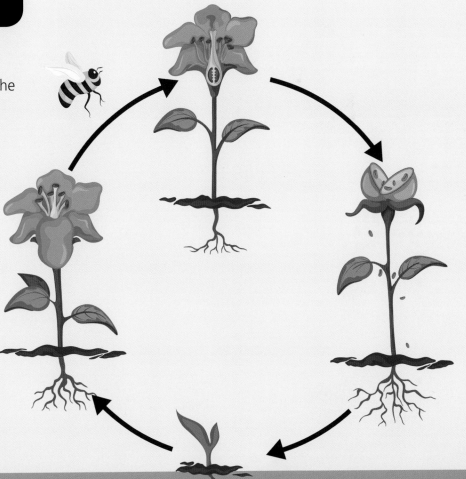

Back from the brink

It is important to protect the biodiversity we still have left. Once species become extinct and habitats are destroyed, they are gone forever.

Saving the environment

Preventing more damage to the environment will help to slow the loss of biodiversity. By switching from fossil fuels to cleaner sources of energy that produce less carbon dioxide, such as wind power, we can stop global warming from getting worse and affecting habitats, such as the poles. We must also reduce and clean up pollution that affects biodiversity, such as plastic in the ocean.

In your hands

Every day, we make choices that affect the environment and biodiversity without even knowing it. The products that we buy and the food that we eat, such as fish from trawler ships, can lead to biodiversity being lost. If possible, try to buy sustainable products that are produced responsibly.

Wildlife reserves

Setting up protected reserves is a good way of preserving biodiversity. People can't build on the land, or gather resources from a protected area, so the species that live there won't be affected by deforestation or pollution. Some protected reserves employ wildlife rangers to protect animals from poachers.

Breeding programs

If the population of a species is decreasing, zoos and conservation projects set up breeding programs. They are bred from endangered species in captivity. A regular food supply and health care helps them survive. The animals are encouraged to hunt and behave as they would in the wild. Some animals are returned to their natural habitats.

Reintroduction

Sometimes, scientists deliberately move animals to certain areas. These animals can help support a population that already exists. In some cases, animals are brought back to an area where they used to live in the past. Bringing back these animals helps to increase biodiversity and can create a balance between predators and prey in the ecosystem.

In 1995, gray wolves were reintroduced to Yellowstone National Park located in Wyoming, Montana, and Idaho. The wolves were native to the area but were hunted out. They were brought back to control the elk population that grew and altered the ecosystem.

Gone forever?

It is possible, in theory, to bring back extinct animals through cloning. Scientists are currently working on mammoths and passenger pigeons, although the process is slow and difficult, and has not yet been successful.

The bald eagle

The bald eagle is America's national bird. However, it almost disappeared because of hunting, habitat destruction, and pesticides.

FACT FILE

LOCATION:
North America

POPULATION IN 1963:
487 nesting pairs

POPULATION IN 2007:
9,789 nesting pairs

Shooting

In the early 1900s, many bald eagles were shot. Some people hunted them for sport. Others believed that bald eagles were dangerous to livestock, so they killed them.

Pesticides

The bald eagle population was seriously affected by the use of a pesticide called DDT in the 1940s and 1950s.

Rising numbers

After DDT was banned in 1972, the bald eagle population started to recover. Over the years, breeding programs have helped numbers to rise further. In 2007, the bald eagle was removed from the list of threatened wildlife. However, they are still protected, so that their population does not drop again.

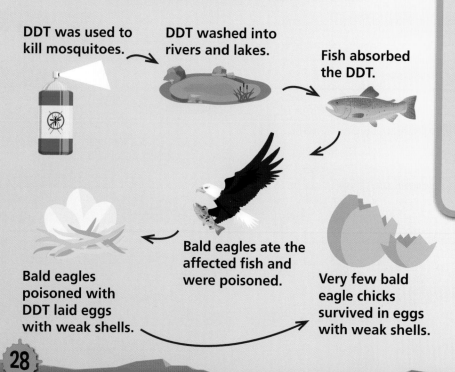

DDT was used to kill mosquitoes.

DDT washed into rivers and lakes.

Fish absorbed the DDT.

Bald eagles ate the affected fish and were poisoned.

Bald eagles poisoned with DDT laid eggs with weak shells.

Very few bald eagle chicks survived in eggs with weak shells.

The bald eagle population dropped, as few chicks were born.

The humpback whale

Humpback whales are a protection success story. Their numbers seriously dropped as a result of hunting, but they were brought back from the brink, thanks to a whaling ban.

FACT FILE

LOCATION:
Worldwide

POPULATION IN 1966:
5,000

POPULATION IN 2018:
80,000

Hunting

Between the 1700s and the early 1900s, humpback whales were almost driven to extinction. They were hunted throughout the world for their meat, their bones, and their fat, which was used in oil lamps.

Whalers used harpoons to catch whales. The whales were then brought back to a larger ship and transported to shore.

The twentieth century

Advances in technology in the 1900s made it much easier to catch humpback whales. The population quickly dropped, as too many were caught. In the 1960s, a worldwide ban on hunting humpback whales was put in place. Since the ban, their population in the wild has recovered significantly.

Current threats

Although most groups of humpback whales around the world have a healthy population, they are still threatened by oil spills and pollution. Loud noises from ships confuse the whales and stop them from resting. They can also get tangled in fishing nets and drown. Solving these problems will help to protect the humpback whale population for the future.

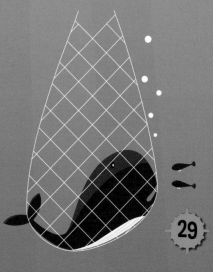

Glossary

boycott To refuse to buy something or to act in a way that shows you do not support it

deforestation Cutting down trees and clearing the land

diversity A range of different things

DNA The genetic information that controls who we are

ecosystem All the living things in an area

erosion The wearing away of soil

extinction When a species of a living thing no longer exists

fertilizer A substance added to plants to make them grow well

fossil fuel A fuel that comes from the ground, such as coal, oil, or gas

global warming The increase of temperature on Earth, partly due to the greenhouse effect

greenhouse gas A gas that traps heat in the atmosphere, such as carbon dioxide

livestock Animals that are raised for their meat or other products

migrate To move to another area, usually at a certain time of year

pesticide A chemical used to kill insects and other living things that harm plants

poaching Illegal hunting

pollinate To transfer pollen from one plant to another, producing seeds

reproduce To produce young (babies)

resistant Not harmed or affected by something

species A kind of plant or animal

sustainable Describes something that can continue for a long time because it does not harm the environment

Learning More

Books

Howell, Izzi. ***Biome Geo Facts.*** Crabtree Publishing, 2018.

Levete, Sarah. ***Habitats and Wildlife in Danger.*** Crabtree Publishing, 2010.

Strauss, Rochelle. ***Tree of Life: The Incredible Biodiversity of Life on Earth.*** Kids Can Press, 2013.

Websites

thekidshouldseethis.com/post/why-is-biodiversity-so-important-ted-ed
Watch a video about biodiversity.

www.amnh.org/explore/ology/biodiversity/endangered-species-game2
Print out a game about protecting endangered species.

www.bbc.co.uk/newsround/37373034
Read about the ivory trade.

Index